SUPER STEM CAREERS

A Day at Work with a
CHEMIST

ROSALIE GADDI

New York

Published in 2016 by The Rosen Publishing Group, Inc.
29 East 21st Street, New York, NY 10010

First Edition

Editor: Caitie McAneney
Book Design: Katelyn Heinle

Photo Credits: Cover Photographee.eu/Shutterstock.com; cover, pp. 1, 3, 4, 6–8, 10–12, 14–16, 18, 20, 22–24 (molecular vector design) phloxii/Shutterstock.com; p. 5 Prasit Rodphan/Shutterstock.com; p. 6 Picsfive/Shutterstock.com; p. 7 Shots Studio/Shutterstock.com; p. 9 Media for Medical/Universal Images Group/Getty Images; p. 11 (main) ggw1962/Shutterstock.com; p. 11 (inset) Africa Studio/Shutterstock.com; p. 13 Steve Allen/Stockbyte/Getty Images; p. 15 RGtimeline/Shutterstock.com; p. 16 Zerbor/Shutterstock.com; p. 17 Matej Kastelic/Shutterstock.com; p. 19 Andrea Danti/Shutterstock.com; p. 21 (top) Tui-PhotoEngineer/Shutterstock.com; p. 21 (bottom) cubephoto/Shutterstock.com; p. 22 Klaus Vedfelt/Taxi/Getty Images.

Library of Congress Cataloging-in-Publication Data

Gaddi, Rosalie, author.
 A day at work with a chemist / Rosalie Gaddi.
    pages cm. — (Super STEM careers)
 Includes index.
 ISBN 978-1-5081-4402-1 (pbk.)
 ISBN 978-1-5081-4403-8 (6 pack)
 ISBN 978-1-5081-4404-5 (library binding)
 1. Chemistry—Vocational guidance—Juvenile literature. 2. Chemists—Juvenile literature.
 I. Title.
 QD39.5.G33 2016
 540—dc23
                              2015023458

Manufactured in the United States of America

CPSIA Compliance Information: Batch #BW16PK: For Further Information contact Rosen Publishing, New York, New York at 1-800-237-9932

CONTENTS

A DAY AT THE LAB

Chemists are scientists who study and test matter to see what it's made of and how it **reacts** with other matter. These scientists usually work in a laboratory setting. However, not all chemists do the same job. They work with different kinds of matter. While some chemists work with medicine, others work to improve products, such as food, plastic, or even fuel. Some work on computers to **develop** ideas and test chemical reactions.

Chemists use STEM in their career every day. "STEM" stands for "science, **technology**, **engineering**, and math." Let's learn more about this exciting STEM career!

SUPER STEM SMARTS

When a chemist works outside the laboratory, it's called working "in the field."

Chemists work with the newest and most advanced technology to study and test matter.

WHAT IS CHEMISTRY?

Chemistry is a branch of science, so chemists use science in their jobs every day! Chemistry is the study of matter and the way it changes. Everything in the world, and even out in space, is made of matter. Anything that takes up space—even the tiniest amount—is matter.

There are five different states of matter, but the most well-known are solid, liquid, and gas. Matter can change from one state to another, which is called a physical change. For example, water is a liquid. When water gets really cold it forms ice, a solid. When water gets really hot, it forms water vapor, a gas.

SUPER STEM SMARTS

When an ice pop melts, it changes from a solid to a liquid. That's a physical change.

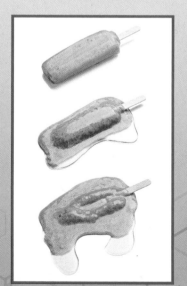

Chemists observe and test different physical changes. They might see what temperature it takes to turn a liquid into a gas.

CHEMICAL CHANGES

Atoms are considered the basic building blocks of matter. They're also the smallest piece of each **element**, such as oxygen or iron, that can exist alone. Two or more atoms stuck together, or bonded, are called a molecule. An example of a molecule is H_2O, which is water. It's made from 2 hydrogen (H) atoms and 1 oxygen (O) atom.

Chemists often combine matter to test the chemical reaction that takes place. A chemical reaction occurs when bonds are broken or created. For example, a chemist might add an extra oxygen atom to a water molecule, which creates H_2O_2, or hydrogen peroxide.

Chemists need to know which molecules are in the matter they're combining. Certain chemical reactions cause explosions or the creation of harmful matter.

BASIC CHEMISTRY TOOLS

When a chemist works in a lab, they have many tools to help them do their job. Many basic chemistry tools have been used for a long time. Chemists need to measure liquids before they combine them. To do so, they use beakers. Beakers are containers with measurement markings on the side. They may also use flasks, which are like beakers with a smaller opening. Test tubes hold smaller amounts of matter.

Chemists sometimes need to measure the mass, or amount of matter, of their **materials**. They can use an electronic scale or a balance to find mass. Some chemists need to heat matter to observe its physical changes. They might use a Bunsen burner, which produces a gas flame.

SUPER STEM SMARTS

Mass is very similar to weight. Mass is the measure of matter in an object, and weight is the measure of how heavy the object is.

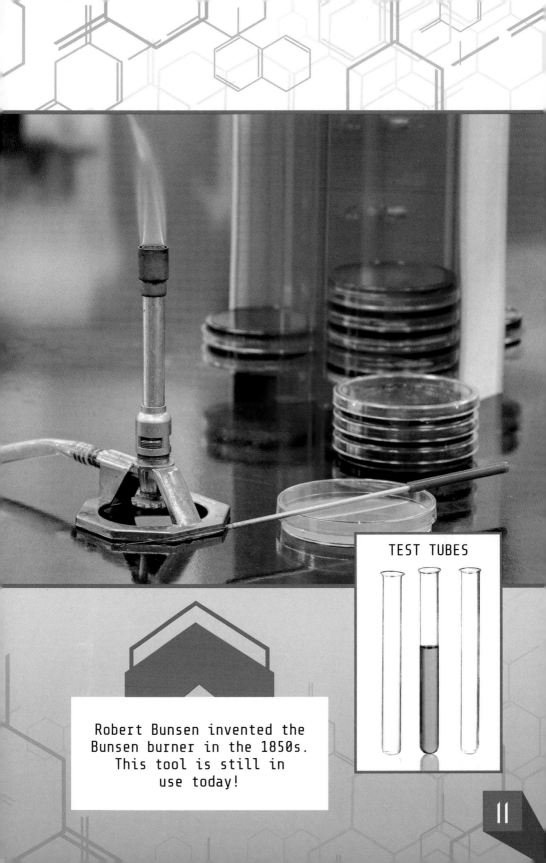

TEST TUBES

Robert Bunsen invented the Bunsen burner in the 1850s. This tool is still in use today!

THE LATEST TECHNOLOGY

Today's chemists depend on computers to do much of their work. A chemist may use computers to study, or research, the properties of a certain kind of matter as well as find experiments and information from other chemists. Computers also allow chemists to record an experiment's results, organize them into charts and graphs, and share them. Some computer programs can **simulate** a chemical reaction, which helps avoid harmful reactions.

Chemists may heat matter with **lasers**, which work more effectively than Bunsen burners. Spectrometers are machines that measure changes in the color of matter.

Chemists use special tools called electron microscopes when they need to look at pieces of matter too tiny to view with a regular microscope. These microscopes use a beam of electrons to create an image that's much sharper and clearer than the images ordinary microscopes create.

BASIC CHEMISTRY TOOLS

- electronic scale
- Bunsen burner
- tongs
- notebook and pen
- goggles
- flask
- beaker
- dropper
- test tube

MODERN CHEMISTRY TOOLS

- spectrometer
- computer
- electron microscope
- laser

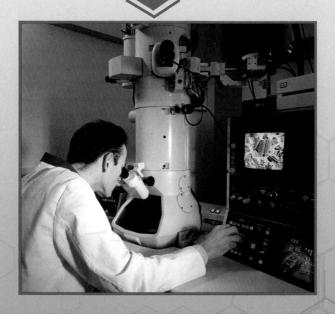

CHEMISTS IN ENGINEERING

Chemists not only use the newest technology—they create it. **Designing**, building, and using materials is called engineering. Some chemists act as engineers when they create new products, from fuel to plastics.

To create a new product, a chemist researches the current products available and the materials used to make them. Imagine a chemist wants to make the plastic on a watch harder and lighter. They'd look for new matter they could add to the plastic to produce a new kind of plastic. After designing the plastic, they'd create it and test it.

SUPER STEM SMARTS

Chemical engineers use life science, physical science, and math in their work. They're good at problem solving and thinking outside of the box.

Chemical engineers are both
scientists and engineers. They
design, plan, and test **equipment**
and processes for manufacturing
a product.

Some chemists engineer new food products. They might test what happens to food as it's stored or prepared. They may try adding chemicals to the food so it lasts longer. They may put additives, or additional matter, into food so it's healthier and safer to eat.

Medicinal chemists have a very important job. They work to develop medicine that will heal certain illnesses. They might discover new matter in nature that has medicinal properties. Or they combine matter to create a whole new drug. They test each medicine to make sure it's safe.

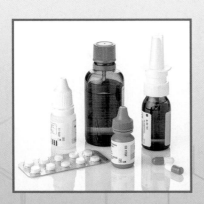

Food and medicinal chemists need to make sure their products are safe and effective.

MATH ON THE JOB

Chemists use math every day. Chemical reactions can be represented by special **equations**. These equations add up the different elements in the molecules. Often, there are more than two molecules, so a chemist needs to keep track of all the numbers. The result of the equation tells a chemist what the chemical reaction will create.

Chemists need to use math to take correct measurements and use them. For example, imagine a chemist measures liquid in a beaker to be 150 milliliters. They need to split this up into 5 equal parts. That's 30 milliliters in each part.

This is the chemical equation for photosynthesis, the process by which a plant makes its food. The first side of the equation adds carbon dioxide and water. With sunlight, this combination produces oxygen and a type of sugar.

SUNLIGHT

OXYGEN

CARBON DIOXIDE

WATER

CARBON DIOXIDE	WATER		SUGAR	OXYGEN

$$6CO_2 + 6H_2O \text{ ---> } C_6H_{12}O_6 + 6O_2$$

SUNLIGHT

DIFFERENT KINDS OF CHEMISTS

What does a chemist do on an average day? That's a hard question, because there are many types of chemists. Many work in a lab, but some work in the field. Some chemists work in schools and colleges. Some create products, while others **analyze** the different properties of matter.

Forensic chemists study **evidence** from crime scenes, such as blood or leftover gunpowder, to help solve crimes. Chemical technicians work in labs to make sure chemical processes and equipment are working well. Environmental chemists observe, collect, and analyze the chemicals in the soil, water, and air.

SUPER STEM SMARTS

Process chemists design the best methods by which a product can be produced on a large scale.

This chemical technician (above) spends most of her day in the lab. However, this environmental chemist (below) is out in the field collecting samples.

BECOMING A CHEMIST

A chemist gets to work with STEM every day. They're able to do experiments and use cool tools, such as microscropes and lasers.

To be a chemist, you need to earn at least a four-year college degree, but most chemists continue their education past that. You can find an **internship** working for a company as a chemist. You can also study computers, biology, math, and engineering.

A job as a chemist is challenging but fun! You can discover new things every day. Whether in a lab or in the field, chemists take a close look at the building blocks of our world and try to make it better.

GLOSSARY

analyze: To study something deeply.

design: To create the plan for something.

develop: To work on something over time.

element: Matter that's pure and has no other type of matter in it.

engineering: The use of science and math to build better objects.

equation: A mathematical statement that two amounts are equal.

equipment: Tools, clothing, and other items needed for a job.

evidence: Something that shows that something else is true.

internship: An educational or training program that gives experience for a career.

laser: A device that produces a thin, powerful beam of light that has many special uses.

material: Something used to make something else.

react: To do something because of something else that happens.

simulate: To represent the operation of a process by means of another system.

technology: The way people do something using tools and the tools that they use.

INDEX

WEBSITES

Due to the changing nature of Internet links, PowerKids Press has developed an online list of websites related to the subject of this book. This site is updated regularly. Please use this link to access the list: www.powerkidslinks.com/ssc/chem